I0442970

The Good, Bad and Ugly of Product Reviews

ASIN – B093DV3CSW

Patrick X. Gallagher

As seen on CBS, FOX, NBC & ABC

v1.6

"Product names, brands, and other trademarks referred to within this book are the property of their respective trademark holders. Unless otherwise specified, no association between the author and any trademark holder is expressed or implied. Use of a term in this book should not be regarded as affecting the validity of any trademark, registered trademark, or service mark."

All rights reserved worldwide

Copyright © 2021-3020

Perception is Reality

"Things are not always what they seem; the first appearance deceives many; the intelligence of a few perceives what has been carefully hidden." -***Phaedrus***

Acknowledgements

This book is dedicated to all the self-published authors who have helped other writers get their content published and reviewed. You have gotten your book out, but now rogue shills are ruining your work, profiting from 1-star reviews.

How can you combat that? Read on to find out more about these unscrupulous Amazon member accounts.

To my wonderful wife, who helped me see what is really good and understand what is truly bad.

Last updated –*April. 2023.*

Table of Contents

Introduction	1
Who this book is for?	7
How to Write a Review on Amazon	9
What to Consider Before Writing the Review	14
How Do Sellers, or Authors Get Reviews?	22
How to Spot Fake Reviews	49
The Authentic Way to Get Reviews	68
8 Easy Ways to Support Your Favorite Author	84
In Conclusion	88
Get Lifetime Updates of This eBook	92
Sources - Further Reading and Products For Review	96
Recommended Websites for Further Review	100
Amazon Terms & Glossary	104
Questions or Comments?	106
Other Books by the Author	108
Now Please Share Your Opinion and Write a Review	110
About the Author	112

Disclaimer

This publication may not be reproduced in any form without prior consent from the author, or publisher.

Prior to publication, all attempts to review accuracy, verification of the information provided has been completed.

This book is intended to inform and is for educational purposes only. You may use and quote up to 100 words from this eBook when writing a review.

Any perceived criticism of any individual, or organization is unintentional.

A Message Interruption by Amazon…

A message from Amazon about reading eBooks listed on Amazon.com for FREE…

You can borrow up to **10 eBooks per month** for no additional expense if you join the Kindle Lending library. The program is known as kindle unlimited. More information can be found here: Click here.

If you are an **Amazon Prime** customer, you can borrow one book per month at no additional charge as well. More information can be sought here: Click here.

What is **Prime Reading Eligible**? Prime Reading is a part of Amazon Prime multi-benefit subscription and offers unlimited access to 1,000 Kindle books, magazines, and comic books.

Kindle Unlimited is a standalone subscription that offers unlimited access to over 1.4 million Kindle books and magazines. Currently you get access to 3 magazines as part of the subscription.

Source: https://ebookfriendly.com/amazon-prime-reading-things-to-know/

Find the current list of eBooks available here. Prime Reading Eligible: http://amzn.to/2B44BZM

Similar Keywords: 1: Fake; 2: Authentic Reviews; 3: Amazon Vine; 4: How to Spot Fake Reviews;

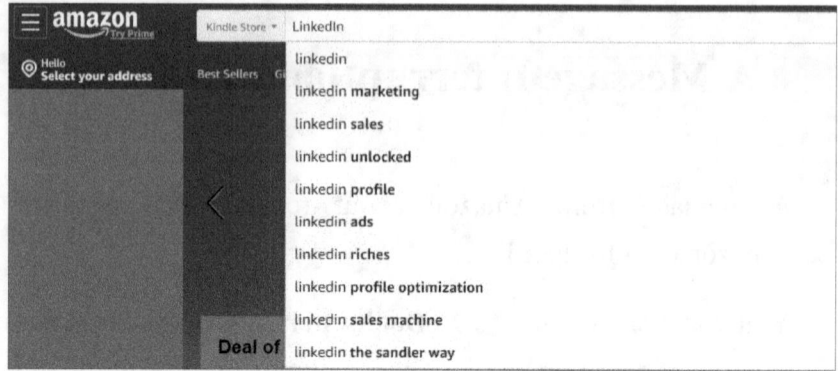

The above screenshot shows what keywords are searched the most on Amazon.com.

This is for authors: You have a great opportunity to sell your eBook when an Amazon customer purchases your paperback. Don't forget to enroll your published book(s) in **Amazon's Kindle Lending Library.**

Introduction

"Spoken words fly away, written words remain."–*Anonymous*

Since the year 2000, I have been giving Amazon money in exchange for them to send me electronics and other goods.

In September 2012, that changed, as Amazon started sending me money too.

After several years of having an account on Amazon, I started writing reviews on those products sold by Amazon which I had received.

Even before then, I was writing letters to major consumer manufacturers about their products.

Like Ideal, long gone now, I waited 5-10 years to buy a TCR set, only to find out on **Christmas Day** that they sent me a dead-on-arrival (DOA) transformer. My total control racing set had no power!

I was calling them on Christmas Day as a child to tell them to fix it, but I was not the only one who had an issue.

Fast forward to today, I know a whole lot more information about product reviews, companies, new product introduction and how publishing works.

I have acted in the roles of new product introduction, author, publisher, writer, product tester and product reviewer.

All these <u>acting roles</u> have helped me get to this point in writing my experience of product reviews.

This Amazon publishing and review platform <u>does not work</u> how you have read or believe that it works. That is until now. **Reading this eBook should change that**.

In fact, this process probably goes way back to thousands of years ago.

Like, **when the first slate was published**. How did they do reviews back then? Word of mouth? Reviews started and were recommended by friends and family.

Still, I don't want to write my take on his-story, as I will never finish this eBook. Let me just start with some bad stuff.

The person who got selected to run **Amazon.com** is known to most people as **Jeff Bezos**. That's not his real name, mind you.

His real name is <u>Jeff Jorgensen</u>. Why can't these people use their real names?

If you take the time to research the genealogy databases, you will come to find out that Jeff's grandfather was **Lawrence Preston Gise**.

Bezos is a Pollack and a Gise, and he now owns part of what used to be the extended <u>King Ranch</u>. His ancestors are Kings! Basically, everything he has, **he inherited!**

At age 30, Jeff Jorgensen apparently came up with the idea to sell books via the internet. His business model that he followed the script for was to sell books by web-order.

Abebooks was already doing business selling books over the internet.

Back in 1994, were books selling on the internet like hotcakes? **No, they were not selling well at all.**

In fact, if you track Amazon's sales in the first **4** to **7** years, the company did not make any money!

2001 was the year that Amazon started to turn a profit. And that was right after the 2000 dot com bust. Abebooks, the company I mentioned earlier, was bought by Amazon in 2008.

More recently, just over 6-7 years ago, **Jeff was supposedly worth 71 billion**. How did he quadruple his wealth from 18 billion in just a few years? Really? **He did all that in a down market?**

This was all while bookstores were going out of business and book sales continued to be in decline.

Then if you look at the man who the media calls Jeff Bezos, watch a video on him.

What has he said that would ever break a snooze?

Jeff appears to be a card-board cut-out, that registers zero on the charisma scale and zero on the reality scale. He is just not that convincing in the role he has been given.

He is pretty good at reading from the teleprompter, and that is about it!

Back to selling and reading books. Books have continued to be <u>read less each year</u> and **book sales continue to be on the decline.**

Now there are even <u>sites</u> that sell students an abbreviated summary of a book.

So, readers don't even read the whole book, or even buy it! A lot of book reviews are written when it is available FREE!

With that in mind, would you expect book reviews to be written with any integrity? Out of all the books sold that have reviews, **what is the percentage of reviews that are authentic?**

Is it 10%, 30%, or 50%, or higher? By the time you get through this eBook, you should have the answer.

Jeff Bezos started the company selling books over the internet, <u>paying people to write reviews</u>. Not much has changed in 20-plus years.

It is in the Terms and Conditions that writing paid reviews is not allowed, and in this eBook, you will see exactly what reviewers are sent to write a review.

Today, reviews are still "fake" and people who write them get paid or are given stuff in exchange for posting them.

Amazon even has a review program called Vine that works on that principle.

In this eBook, you are going to find out **the good, the bad** and **the ugly** of product reviews. It is mostly focused on book reviews.

You will also get real emails that I have been sent that request me to write reviews.

I am a member of the *Amazon *Vine Review Program*. This is an invitation-only review membership program. I do not write 5-star reviews 100% of the time. My reviewer ranking is currently at 92%.

I am not sure why I got selected to the **Vine Review Program**, but I still stay true to myself. I do not write fake reviews, even if I get the product for free.

You will also find out how reviews are gotten, even before a book is published. I will share first-hand experience how ugly the review process is, even after Amazon received bad press about it.

For me, authentic reviews are this: the only way you can get an authentic review is not to ask for one, period. In the next section, I will explain who this book is for.

*Vine: This customer is a member of Amazon Vine™ Voice, an invitation only program that gives Amazon reviewers advance access to not-yet-released products for the purpose of writing reviews. A review written as part of the Vine™ Voice program always includes this label: "Amazon Vine™ Review" on the initial product detail page and "Customer review from the Amazon Vine™ Program" when viewing the entire review. This is a permanent badge.

Here is my rating for this section.

My Good, Bad, or Ugly rating: Bad	Why?
THE BAD	-Books are continuing to be read less each year -Bezos started the company paying people to write reviews -People don't read books cover-to-cover, so how can they write a good review? -Amazon has an influence review program, called Vine. Products are given free in the exchange of a review

Who This eBook Is For?

"Most books reviews aren't very well-written. They tend to be more about the reviewer than the book." -*Tibor Fischer*

This table below should help you figure out very quickly if you should read this eBook.

Is For	Is Not For
Small-Publishers/Self-Published Authors	Mainstream publishers
Critical Thinkers	People who criticize with-out thinking
Amazon Authentic Reviewers	Shill Reviewers
	Those that profit from dropping 1-star reviews
	Readers that believe J.K. Rowling is an author
	People who pay for reviews
	Amazon **Verified Reviewers** who write a review and get reimbursed for their purchases
	People who are experts on the Amazon review system
	You cannot see what opportunity you have inside of you already

As you can see from the table, the target audience for this book is quite small.

However, the target audience is for those that want to receive authentic reviews, as well as write them.

Would you like to buy all of these, or just this eBook?

How to Write a Review on Amazon

"The Competition and Markets Authority believes that £23bn of online shopping in the UK is influenced by reviews"
–BBC News

Amazon Review Eligibility

You can write a review on a product or eBook you didn't buy on Amazon.com! However, before you can write your first review there are some eligibility requirements. These are listed below.

You must have spent $50 (40 pounds in the UK) with a valid payment card. Gift cards and promotional discounts are not included. Additionally, …

Purchase(s) must have been made in the last 12 months at the time of writing the review

You must have an account with Amazon

You must have a valid email address with Amazon

When writing reviews about products be careful about entering information about shipping, or packaging, or prices. For packaging issues, you can submit feedback via this link:

I recommend you don't write about the packaging, shipping, or price information in your review.

This is to avoid the delay in getting your review posted. You may get an email denying your review and the boiler plate email response does not tell you what specifically got your review denied.

For more information about Amazon eligibility you can go here: https://www.amazon.com/gp/help/customer/display.html?nodeId=201929730

For third party sellers, you can leave feedback on them here: https://www.amazon.com/hz/feedback

In the UK it would be: https://www.amazon.co.uk/hz/feedback

Recommended Review Tips

You start by writing what you liked and end with what you don't like. I recommend that you put one sentence in your review paragraph that you can leverage for your review title.

Three Important Parts

There are 3 important parts to writing the review.

They are: **Review Title**, **Review Body** and **Review Rating**.

You get a bonus review by including a photo, or a video. Very few eBook review ratings have a photo, or even a video.

You can get thumbs up from readers of your review if you take a photo of the book. If it's a product and you are pointing out something good, you can take a picture and upload that.

Make it part of telling the story connecting it with what you are writing.

Best Review Writers

The best review writers will always end with a remark on what the author can improve upon. Kind of like a call to action in sales copy.

Even if the reader loved the eBook there should be an opportunity to improve upon the next version of the eBook.

An eBook reviewer may also end with why they are recommending the eBook.

If you want a list of those Amazon accounts are, you can find them here: https://www.amazon.com/review/top-reviewers

Keep in mind that when you focus on the detail, you will see that a lot of these "top-reviewers" write 5 Star reviews on crap products!

This is my opinion, and therefore I recommend you look at each review to determine what is "good" or "bad" for yourself. Your filter for what is good or bad may be different to mine.

Quoting the eBook

For this eBook, you may quote part of the eBook in your review, but don't quote a whole paragraph to make a point.

Some authors have added a disclaimer on what you can include for reviews, so be aware of that request. Check first before you assume it's ok to quote the book.

Bonus Review Tip

Insert a link to another product on Amazon. This is useful if you want to refer the reader to a product that you found that may be better.

I use this technique also in another way for some reviews of books I have read.

It's also a good way to recommend a better product if applicable when writing a review. This may help the reviewer get a "helpful" vote.

Here is what the review form looks like on Amazon USA site.

Review your purchase

The Key Factor: Understanding the Employer's Perspective on Hiring

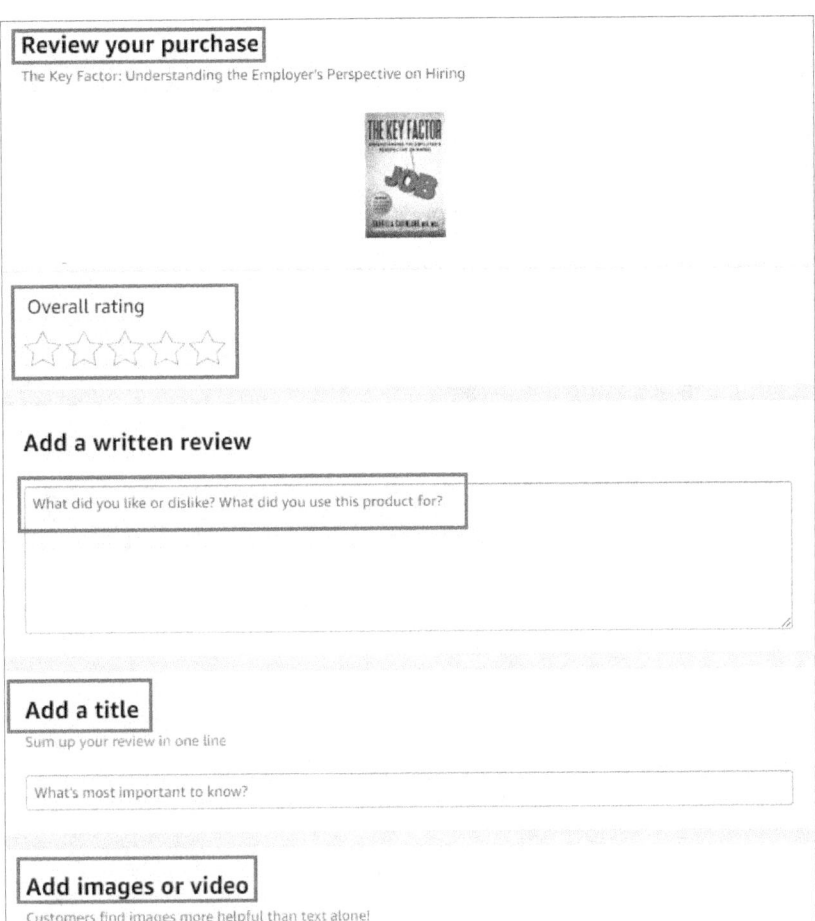

Overall rating

☆☆☆☆☆

Add a written review

What did you like or dislike? What did you use this product for?

Add a title

Sum up your review in one line

What's most important to know?

Add images or video

Customers find images more helpful than text alone!

What to Consider Before Writing the Review

Use a spell-checker for the words you will write.

Did the eBook cover what it talked about in the Book Description?

Was the eBook helpful?

What did I learn?

Were there enough screenshots, or diagrams?

Were the chapters too long?

Did the eBook leave me wanting to know more, or feeling disappointed?

Was the eBook up to date?

Was the eBook targeted to the right audience?

Why would someone want to buy this eBook?

What was missing?

For the product review, is it not as described?

Example Review

Overall Rating: **** (4 stars)

Review Title: Useful Insights

Written Review:

I downloaded this book interested in tips concerning Amazon ranking in general, not LinkedIn Best-Sellers in particular.

I learned quite a few interesting facts, some of them I would have loved to know a few months ago when publishing an eBook for the first time. Others are interesting as a reader as well, like for example how to ensure you will receive future version updates.

The book is concise and easy to follow, yet I found the introduction and the end part tedious. The first part, approx. 20% is taken by acknowledgements, references, definitions etc. and nearly put me off. The part I valued is concentrated in the "How To" chapters.

If you would like to write a review for this eBook, then take a look at what I have gotten started.

Example you could write for this eBook.

Review Title: Book Reviews Are Hard to Read

Overall Rating: **** (4 Stars)

Written Review:

That could be one example for this eBook review. The eBook covered all the items in the book description. Overall, it was very useful to learn. Now I know what to look for in a book, or product review.

After you have written the review, you can then hit the submit button.

Here is a link to the **creating a review of this eBook**, so you can practice writing a review for this eBook! Link: [<u>click, or tap this amazon link here</u>]

Here is another example review.

If you wish to find this review you may search for keywords: "**World without Cancer**" on Amazon.com. At the time of writing this eBook, the review below had 252 helpful votes.

Overall Rating: **** (5 stars)

Review Title: Don't believe a word I said - go find out what is true for yourself

Written Review:

We live in a complex world, but how complex is it really? Most problems can be cured with a simple answer. Is Cancer an over complicated disease introduced to the human population that can be solved by simple instructions? Or is it simply a Business?

Read on to find out for yourself. I recommend this book based on the following quotes...

"Monkeys and other primates at the zoo when given a fresh peach, or apricot will carefully pull away the fleshy part, crack open the hard pit, and devour the seed that remains. Instinct compels them to do this even though they have never seen that kind of fruit before. These seeds are one of the most concentrated sources of nitrilosides to be found anywhere in nature."

Page 58

"It is significant that one seldom finds cancer in the carcasses of the wild animals killed in the hunt. The creatures contract the disease only when they are domesticated by man and forced to eat the food he produces or the scraps from his table."

Foods that are high in Nitriloside: Millet, Apricot and peach

Page 60

An apple a day keeps the doctor a way...could have been more of an idle slogan...the apple seeds are high in vitamin B17.

Page 61:

And God said: Behold I have given you every herb-bearing seed upon the earth, and all trees that have in themselves seed of their own kind, to be your meat. (Genesis 1:29)

Page 63: Chapter - The Ultimate Test

The best way to prove or disprove the vitamin theory of cancer would be to take a large group of people numbering in the thousands, and over a period of many years, expose them to a diet of rich nitrilside foods, and then check the results. This surely would be the ultimate test.

Update: Nov. 2017 - This book changed my life. I feel that I now know the secret to life longevity. Thank you for all those that voted up this review!

Update May 2018 - My tip: Get fresh peaches and put all the pitts together in a plastic bag and extract the seed inside (use a hammer to crack them). That way you will have fresh B17 that you can put into your body when you are ready to do so.

Recommended Further Reading:

- Salt Your Way to Health, 2nd Edition
- The Great Cholesterol Myth: Why Lowering Your Cholesterol Won't Prevent Heart Disease-and the Statin-Free Plan That Will
- The High Blood Pressure Hoax
- You're Not Fat You're Toxic, Your Permanent Weight Loss Program
- The Prevention of All Cancers

Don't believe a word I said - go find out what is true for yourself by reading the work of the author.

Here are some other 3-star review ratings that are <u>unhelpful</u> for the same book: World Without Cancer; The Story of Vitamin B17

Review Title: Three Stars

Written Review: JUST OK

Review Title: Three Stars

Written Review: ITS IS OK

Review Title: Maybe later

Written Review: Ok, haven't finished reading

These reviews are not at all helpful to a potential buyer of the book! Consequently, the reviewer had no "Helpful" votes.

The book had 560 global ratings and an average star rating of 4.7.

What do the Overall rating stars mean?

You can see from the graphics following, how these ratings should be interpreted. This is the same for books, or products.

I find reviewers and especially raters, do not understand what the stars mean! Yes, they just press or tap a button on the screen!

Case Studies

In this section I am going to take a look at some reviews that you should look for and those that you should ignore too.

Two important steps. 1) Filter all the review on verified reviews first. 2) Filter out any Vine Reviews and because you filtered on verified reviews you won't see any non-purchases, like the Kindle Unlimited reviews.

Pre-Order Reviews

On Amazon you can review a book you haven't even purchased on Amazon and is not available to buy on Amazon! These are called "Pre-Order" books. The screenshot is from a book that will go on general sale May 2nd.

At the time of writing this eBook, it had **215 reviews** and you could not even buy the book.

Pre-Order Page of a Book

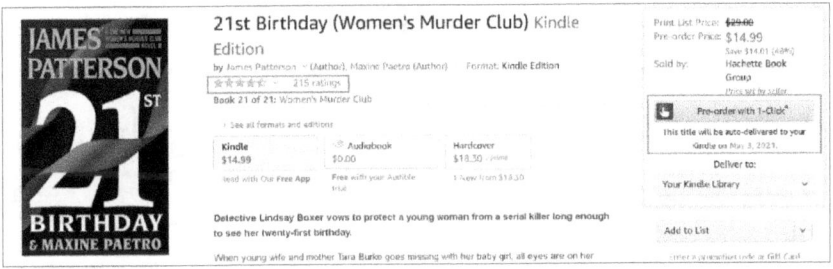

What does that tell you? It tells me that most of the reviews are fake. Let's just be cautious here and say, 50% of the reviews are fake because that's just a given without doing the research!

7 Reasons Why Buyers Do Not Leave a Rating

Here are seven reasons why reviews are not left on Amazon.

1. They do not have an account on Amazon
2. They have not made the minimum purchase requirement (varies per country)
3. Fear
4. They prefer not to have an online social foot-print
5. They do not have anything good to say about the product
6. They despise the brand Amazon – various reasons
7. They do not know how to write, or leave a review

There may be many more answers to why people do not leave reviews on Amazon, but those answers above are the most obvious mentioned by authors and other product sellers.

How Do Sellers, or Authors Get Reviews?

"Amazon is <u>the everything</u> online store where you can buy fake goods. eBay is the online store where you can buy stolen goods." -*Patrick X. Gallagher*

How mainstream publishers do it

Let's take an example of an author that has published 70+ books and has appeared on the New York Best Seller's List once, or twice.

The author agrees with the publisher in their book deal…they ask for a set number of signing books as part of the deal. Let's say 200 to 500 books are granted.

Watch the movie Ghost Writer for a glimpse of how it works (Hollywood style).

Those books are then used to get reviews early, or in some cases even before the book is published. How?

The author will have a mailing (old school), or email list. He/she sends out an email to the list…**I am excited to let you know that I have launched (or I am about to launch) my new book.**

Since you are so <u>great</u>, I am going to give it to you for free.

The book was already given to the author for free and now they are passing it on to the readers. That is great – right? All you must do is send me $10 to cover shipping and I will send it to you.

The author will send your book by media mail, so he/she will make around $7 per book shipped.

He/she will also get your name, address, and email, which can be worth up to $25 per person to the avid sales/Marketer.

The author can then promote their list, or have some other author get their book promoted to the list I just talked about.

Then they will share your email with another publisher, author, or product owner!

Here is an example of a new book pre-launch email. I have changed the name of the sender. The spelling, grammar mechanics have intentionally not been corrected.

YOU did it - "BestBookOnAmazon" just hit amazon #6 bestseller status...

Here's the cheesy link to check right now (updated hourly)

Can you help spread the word and push this little book over the top to #1?

If you pre-order the book today, you will get a TON of high-value business-building bonuses RIGHT NOW and LATER, you'll also get a minty-fresh book jam-packed with savvy marketing, sales and business development strategies, tactics and tools.

(You'll be among the first to take delivery of the book the moment it is released - on or about Jan. 7)

To check out the pre-order bonuses you'll get immediately when you buy today, visit:

http://helpmeoutplease.com/book

I'd love your help in topping the amazon charts today - even before the book is released.

Is it a good book? Obviously, I think so... but fortunately, I'm not alone! Here are just a few other people's opinions...

===

"Insert review 1"

"Insert review 2"

"Insert review 3"

"Insert review 4"

I'll keep you updated on how we do on this.

Will we hit #1?

With YOUR help, I know we can!

But by then, YOU will already be working your way through all the bonus goodies plus your 21-Day Reviewer Playbook which you're getting when you pre-order it today.

-- Marketer

p.s. Why should you buy today even though the book won't be out until January? Because in addition to the great bonuses you'll get immediately when you pre-order today, you will also be invited to a series of private webinars, you'll get pre-order only bonus eBooks such as the Do It! So pre-order the book today and then pop over to http://helpmeoutplease.com/book to claim all your goodies.

Thank YOU in advance for your help!

That email message sent to the Author's list above is just one email for a book that hasn't even launched yet on Amazon!

Here is another pre-order email request for a book.

My next book, Great Leaders Don't Follow the Rules: Contrarian Leadership Principles to Transform Your Team and Business comes out in a couple of weeks on <<insert date>>.

Every publisher but one said it was too controversial to publish. But fortunately, I sent it to some friends who seem to like it:

JOHN C. MAXWELL, "Author Kevin gives practical advice for leading in a world that will never be the same."

KEN BLANCHARD, "The author Kevin has discovered gold. Kevin will keep you amused, interested, and motivated...Read this book."

STEPHEN M.R. COVEY, "This book teaches leaders how to reach new levels of success."

You can now pre-order the book and get incredible bonuses but the offer ENDS soon...so don't wait!

MY OFFER: Pre-order just ONE copy before <<insert date>>, you'll receive:

LEADx Leadership Academy: Become a Super Manager with this 3-month subscription to 100+ courses & AI-powered executive coach ($90 value)

Write Your Own Bestseller This Year, in Just 2 Hours Per Week: In this webinar, I'll reveal my exact method for writing quality books in record time and I'll answer all of your book writing and marketing questions ($120 value)

15 Secrets Successful People Know About Time Management by Kevin Kruse: Get both the eBook &audio book versions ($20 value)

Employee Engagement 2.0 by Kevin Kruse: Get both the eBook &audio book versions ($15 value)

Employee Engagement For Everyone by Kevin Kruse: Get the eBook ($5 value)

Click here (or outside the US click here) to pre-order 1 copy, then email your receipt to jackie@leadxxx.org with "Preorder 1" in the subject.

IF YOU PRE-ORDER 10 copies before <<insert date>>, you'll receive:

10 copies of everything in the 1-book package

Great Leaders LIVE 2019: Join Kevin as he leads this 1-day transformational leadership workshop in Philadelphia (October 2019—recordings for those who can't attend in person) ($1000 value)

VIP Mastermind Group: Gain access to the private LEADx group on Facebook

Click here to pre-order 10 copies, then email your receipt to jackie@leadxxx.org with "Preorder 10" in the subject.

IF YOU PRE-ORDER 100 copies before APRIL 2, 2019 you'll receive:

Everything in the above package

Private Web-based training for your team: Kevin will host a live virtual private training session (45 minutes) for your organization on a topic of your choice—Contrarian Leadership, Employee Engagement, Extreme Productivity or AI in Human Resources ($7500 value)

Click here to pre-order 100 copies, then email your receipt to jackie@leadxxx.org with "Preorder 100" in the subject.

CHOOSE YOUR OWN BONUS

Want to order more than 100 copies? Let me know and we can get you a great bulk order discount and creatively come up with a bonus.

And you can buy your pre-orders from anywhere including Amazon, Outside the US Amazon, B&N, 800-CEO-READ, Indiebound, Google Play, iBooks, Book Depository with free worldwide delivery.

Craziest bundle deal I've ever done, hope you enjoy the value and thanks for the pre-order!

What a load of FREE stuff, boy are you going to jump through some hoops to get that – right?

If you are about to publish a book you might even want to snag the template yourself.

Here is another one, where the author is offering the book for FREE, but you have to pay $9.95 in shipping costs to get it. That assumes you are in the USA!

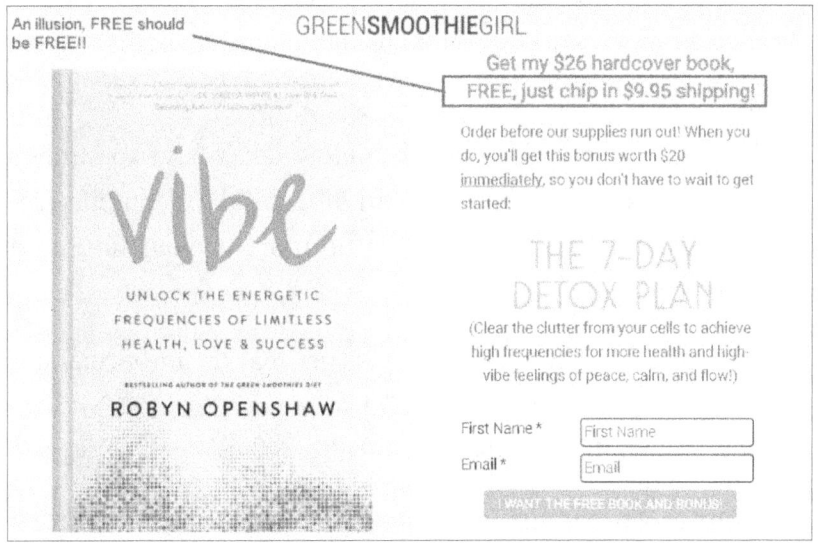

Why do authors do that? There must be a reason! It may be because they will hit some bestseller list, as it counts towards a sale! More information here: https://www.entrepreneur.com/article/244881

This one is from a self-published author.

Hey there!

I'm Robert, an author and a big fan of people like you, who do so much for our community.

I've got a great new book out that seems to be similar to another book you already read and wrote a review for. It's called 'Outsourcing: The Beginners' Guide to Hiring Virtual Assistants'. Here's a short description:

"Are you working hard, trying desperately to get everything done in your business, from communicating with clients and tackling dull admin to working through marketing, email lists and social media accounts?

The great news is that you absolutely don't have to struggle any longer. By simply outsourcing all of that dull or complicated work to a virtual assistant, you'll free up more of your time to do the things that really count.

I've written this book to help you get that dream virtual assistant who can wave their magic wand over your business and be there when you really need them.

I'll guide you through everything you need to know, from writing and posting that job ad, to working together with your brand-new virtual assistant."

Here's a link to the book if you'd like to read the full description and previous reviews:

https://www.amazon.com/dp/linktoeBook (this is not a link that exists at Amazon.com)

If you're available, I'd love to send a free digital copy of the book for you to read and review. Is this the best email address to send it to?

I hope you can check it out. It would give me a small bit of joy in my dark and dreary writer's cave!

Thanks, so much for reading. I hope to hear back from you soon.

Regards,

Message ends.

Here is how another person gets free products from Amazon, by writing FAKE REVIEWs...in his own words:

It's shady but I'm going to show you step by step on how to get free items on Amazon by writing reviews!

So many companies are trying to improve their organic search results and customers benefit by getting a free product in exchange for purchase and reviews.

He starts off with "shady" but continues to engage in the practice!

These are the shady steps.

The steps are simple:

1. Contact the company advertising for a free product on Facebook
2. Buy the product
3. Send them the order number
4. Write a review

5. Tell the company your review is live

6. Receive your money through PayPal

The problem is rampant and similar to fake news on other social media platforms, this is one that Amazon must solve, but probably never will, as they want to continue making a profit.

So, I have just given you some examples of how successful authors get more reviews of their books. You won't see this information published in an eBook like below.

How a small publishing company got reviews.

This person sent me a review request using the following email template. They also used a tool to scrape Amazon for email addresses. This is a subscription-based software program that works on the amount of email addresses returned.

I also interviewed the author/publisher to find out how they got started.

Feel free to use this template. **It worked on me as an Amazon Vine Reviewer.**

Insert template from Peter I.

Email Subject: Do fish spend wisely?

Start of Message

Ahoy,

I'm Peter, and I am the founder of [set name]! publishing company.

I am sure you have received similar emails before. But before you attempt to delete this, you should know that at the end of this email is a picture of a fish trying to spend wisely.

I found you on a list of people who left valuable reviews on As A Man Thinketh (Annotated with Biography about James Allen). This leads me to the reason for this email.

Coronavirus crisis means people are losing their income, yet the bills are still coming.

To help people I wrote a book under a pen name Dana Wise: Save Money and Spend Wisely During and After the Economic Crisis.

In the book, you will discover new ways to enrich your life without spending, how to reach financial freedom by taking steps toward your goals, how to start saving today, and what are good habits of people who are smart with their finances.

I am from Slovakia, a small country in Central Europe, which is about the same size as West Virginia.

Since I am not a native English speaker, I worked with a professional writer and editor from the US.

This extra effort improved the book dramatically as we could combine our certificates, knowledge, and experience in the financial area.

It's difficult for small publishing companies to make an impact because we don't have a huge marketing budget. For us, the best way to become visible is to get honest reviews on Amazon.

Would you like me to send you the book for free? If so, just send me a reply. If not, feel free to tear this email into a thousand pieces or unsubscribe below.

May your day be sunny and filled with great friends.

Peter

End of message

Here is another example. When I looked at the eBook product page it already had greater than 500 reviews!

Start of Promo Request email.

Email Title: **Special Book Bonus for Jamie!**

What's the Bonus?

Before the shutdowns, Jamie spoke at my INFLUENCER event in San Diego, sharing private insights and her best advice from her journey going from **waitress to billion-dollar business builder**.

We've never released her recording from the event, but if you support her book by Friday at midnight, I'll send you access to watch her incredible presentation. Just do this:

1. Order Jamie's book on Amazon by midnight Friday right here.

2. Email your receipt to [email address - edited out]. YES, any Amazon order is fine, from any country and from any day since it's release, as long as it's a PURCHASED order by Friday midnight, in hardcover, Kindle or Audible. (No, free Audible credit claims do not count - only purchased orders).

Sorry ONLY Amazon orders accepted for this promotion we can't check others.

I'll email you the link to her presentation on Saturday once we've seen your receipt!

If you've been trying to rekindle belief in yourself, your dreams, and your future, then you'll LOVE this book! Go get it!

Link to eBook here: https://amzn.to/3qycejT **or here:** https://www.amazon.com/Believe-How-Go-Underestimated-Unstoppable-ebook/dp/B08BZWKPBN

End of Promo Request email.

Here is the actual product page at time of writing.

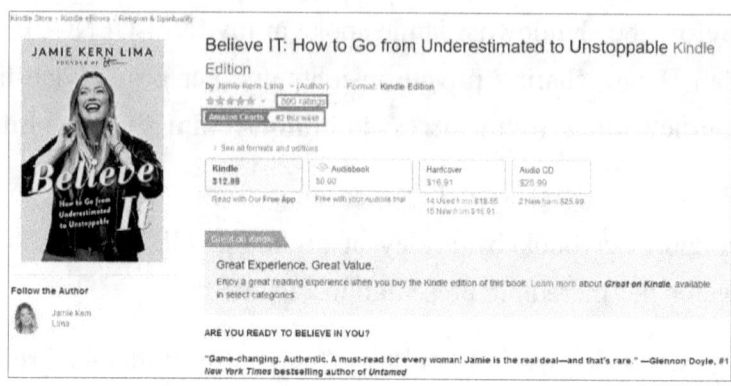

What are some other ways authors, or sellers get reviews?

Below I have listed the remaining examples of soliciting reviews in an un-authentic way.

Joint Authorship Publishing Projects

This idea will come from a small publisher who will send out a call for action to its email list. The call to action will be: We would like to publish a new book and have you be the author.

A collection of authors on the email list will sign-up and then each author writes a chapter, or part of the content. Then that author can send a request to their own email list to get reviews written.

Here's a good example:

Sourced from Amazon.com in March 2021.

What do you notice from the screenshot above?

Let me tell you what I see.

1. The book has multiple authors listed. In this book listing example, it has a total of 11 authors
2. #1 Best Seller – March 18th, 2021
3. 63 Reviews (63 Global Ratings | 56 global reviews)
4. 5 out of 5 – 5-star ratings. 5-star rating percentage is 100%
5. Low price-point $0.99
6. Publication date March 2, 2021
7. 1st review written on March 2, 2021
8. 14 reviews were not "Verified" which could mean they used Kindle Unlimited, or received a pre-launch copy

Now taking all that into consideration, greater than 50% of the reviews were written on the same day of the book being published.

Are you telling me that 30+ readers read 323 pages the same day the book went live on Amazon? No. Remember most people don't read books, **let alone 323 pages in less than 24 hours.**

Therefore, almost all these reviews are probably not authentic. The publisher and authors asked their list to write reviews in exchange for something.

Add to that, there are no other ratings. **No book, or product is 100% perfect.**

My usual Good, Bad, or Ugly summary is below.

My Good, Bad, or Ugly rating: Bad	Why?
	-50% of the reviews were written on the same day -14 unverified reviews – probably received a FREE launch pre-view copy of the book -All 5-Star Ratings (Average Good rating is 4.6)

Social Media Review Requests

This final review request is for products. I get quite a few from LinkedIn. I have copied the InMail sent to my LinkedIn account below.

Email Review Request

Dear friend,

It's Angelina, I got your email from the old customer list.

We have new products on Amazon: Candle lighter

Are you interested in participating in product testing? You can choose one of them to test.

Now this product is in the testing phase, we would like to invite you to try our product and leave a review for this product.

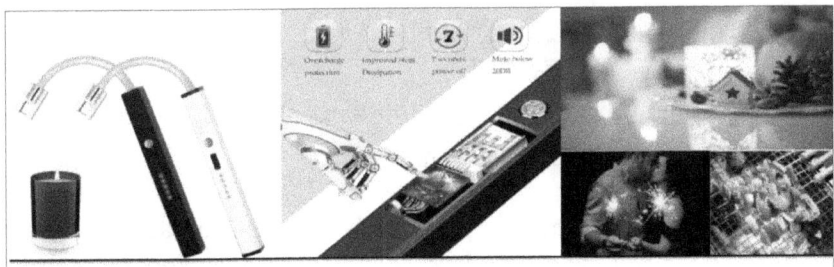

Candle lighter(2 Pack)
- USB Rechargeable lighter(Type C, Faster Charging)
- Longer Than Other Sellers; Quieter during ignition
- No Gas, No Fluid required
- Windproof Flameless Design
- Perfect for Kitchen, BBQ, Outdoor, Party and more

We would like to improve more high-quality and low-price products for customers.

Your advice will help more customers and ourselves understand the products.

No worries, it's all free. If you are interested, please reply to this email directly and we will reply to you within 24 hours.

Looking forward to your reply.

This reviewer requestor or seller was sneaky, as they used a seller's list of emails they got from somewhere.

I know as the email I received this at is only used for product purchases I make via FBA (Fulfilled by Amazon).

I am not going to review their products! They will probably be doing the old PayPal scheme.

Buy it, then leave a review and we will refund your money, regardless of the product quality and oh yeah, it has to be a 5 Star review.

Amazon Vine Program

My take on this is from my experience in being part of this review program run by Amazon. What is it?

Basically, this is the one process that violates an authentic review. All Vine reviews should be looked at with a skeptical eye. Why?

Those that write the reviews are receiving a free product in exchange for a review.

You can find out more about this program from the outside here: https://www.amazon.com/gp/vine/help

From the inside, once you have been asked to join and you choose to join you have to fill in some paperwork. Originally you did not have to give tax information away, but today you do.

That means for US taxpayers, once a year all of the free products you have received and may have written a review have a taxable value.

When you have filled in the paperwork you will be able to receive free products. On the next page, you will see how this appears to a US Vine Program member.

In most cases the taxable value is less than the current retail value.

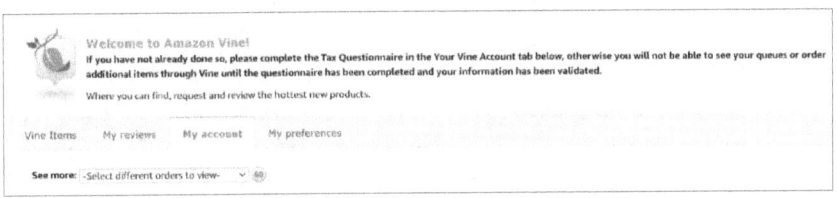

Starting from the left, there are 4 dashboard items for the Vine program. These are: **Vine Items**, **My reviews**, **My account**, and **My preferences**.

I will describe what each of these do for the Vine Program member.

Vine Items: When you click this from the dashboard it divides the number of available items for review into 3 categories. These are: Recommended for you (based on your pre-configured preferences, called "My preferences", Available for all, Additional items.

When you click on "Available for all" it will show the total number of items to review in the US market. At the time of writing there were 3,124 items. This is less than "Additional items".

These are divided into further buckets/categories. There are 20. For example, one category is **Clothing, shoes and Jewelry (1483)**. This is the category that has the most items in.

Recommended for you: This has all the items in it bases on your "My preferences".

Additional Items: This shows everything on Amazon that is part of the Amazon Vine Program. At the time of writing there were **21,258 items available to order for FREE** and optionally write a review for!

My reviews: This has two sub-categories. They are Items Awaiting Review and Reviewed Items.

Items Awaiting Review: Any products you have ordered and have not written a review will be listed here. There is a little gold button that says. Review this product. When you click it, it will take you to the product listing review panel. Then you can write the review.

Reviewed Items: This category will list all the Vine Program Items you received with a link to the review you wrote. It will say, "Review Complete" in green with a button on the right to edit your review.

My Account: This has a link to the Tax documents. The following information is listed in this section, which I will not elaborate on further.

Read our Tax FAQ: https://www.amazon.com/gp/vine/faq#tax

Tax Questionnaire Status: If you have completed it and it has been validated it will say: **Completed**/Validated.

Tax Questionnaire: This is a link to the questions. On that page there is a link to the questions, forms delivery options, and a contact us button. The questionnaire is listed as: Start/Update Questionnaire.

Here is a link: https://www.amazon.com/gp/vine/tax-interview/landing

Estimated Tax Value: For each year you have been using Amazon Vine, there will be a year quoted with the estimated tax value. Depending on which country you are in it will list the currency amount.

Itemized Order Report: For each year you have been a member of the Amazon Vine Program their will be a link to the report. When you click the link it will open up a pdf report.

Here is a link to that section:
https://www.amazon.com/gp/vine/tax-report?year=2020

Where's My Free Stuff: This gives you access to all the orders you have placed by year. Just click the corresponding year category.

The link appears here: https://www.amazon.com/gp/vine/request-status

Account Settings: This is further divided into 3 sections as below. Email subscription, Vine Badge, and opt out of the Vine Program.

Email Subscription: There is a link to change your email settings. The only setting you can change is to enable the Vine Program Newsletter email.

Lastly at the bottom of the page you have the options to view and track recent product requests, contact the Vine Program team, and Need help.

This is what a Vine Review looks like on Amazon. In this case it's for an electronic product – a Mouse.

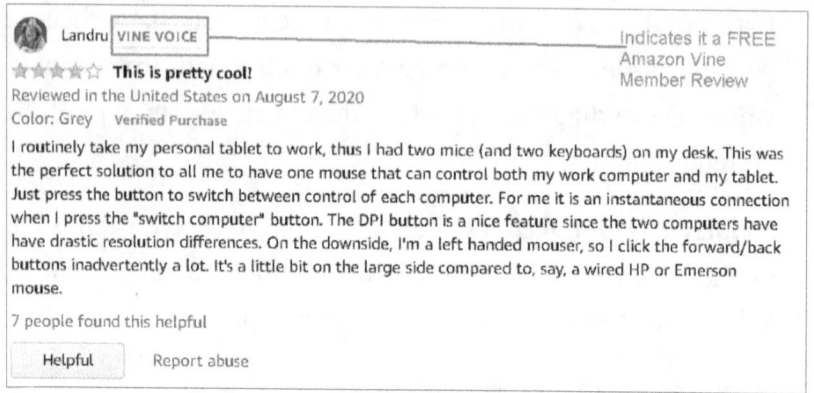

You will notice it has 7 people that voted it helpful. You can see all the reviews for this product here: https://www.amazon.com/gp/product/B082HLRMMH

How Authors Typically Receive Reviews

1.) **They ask for them:** Ask friends, family, colleagues, but make sure you brush up on the Amazon terms and conditions for reviews.

Here is the link again: https://www.amazon.com/gp/help/customer/display.html?nodeId=G3UA5WC5S5UUKB5G

2.) **Authors don't ask for them: This is the best way to get authentic reviews**, but few authors or sellers will follow this recommendation, as everyone out there says you cannot sell something without reviews – I disagree. Just let the content sell for you via word-of-mouth. If you want to get your first review, perhaps you could ask someone you know.

3.) **They get them from Trolls or Shills**. These are the Amazon reviewers who hate your book, or product's success, or are your competition. Maybe they admire it?

4.) **Pre-Launch Marketing**: This is a good one. Most successful authors will have a list of people that will give them a review even before the books is finished or published. Large publishers have an army of them, including some newspaper/media giants. I have included a lot of examples in this chapter.

Here are some example authors that get their reviews that way: Kevin Kruse, Brian Tracy, Timothy Ferriss, Greig Wells, and many more.

5.) **They offer something in Exchange for an honest review**: Go back to the real examples above and you can see how this works. However, for this to work, you must have an email list already.

Here is an example from one 3-star review – "Josh (undoubtedly with help from his **affiliate marketing network**) is obviously a master of sales as he is great at **offering incentives to purchase the book**, as well **as incentives just to write a review**." -**Andrea Hewett**, Amazon Reviewer.

6.) **Someone buys their book or product and leaves the review**: This is another great way to get reviews. Probably most readers (not authors), this is how book reviews are accomplished. How do you get them? Write great content, sell a great product and promote your product through internet channels you will have already pre-wired

7.) **The real ugly:** Pay someone to leave you a review. This can be via sites like, Fiverr, Elance, or Odesk. There are some other variants of this pay model. You can create a competition on your blog and offer readers to send in their receipts as well as a review link to win some money. I know an author who I met for coffee that got 200 reviews that way. Amazon never removed the reviews

8.) **PayPal Solicitations via Social Media:** Another way is for you reach out to potential buyers to buy your product, leave a 5-star review and once the review has posted your money is refunded. I shared an online YouTube video where a young blogger explains how it works.

I have also included some examples in this eBook that I have received to my email inbox.

9.) **Amazon Vine**: You contact Amazon to conduct and participate in the Amazon Vine Program. More details about that program is researched and shared later in this eBook. As you know I am in that program, as requested by Amazon (you cannot ask to join) and I will share inside knowledge of it.

10.) **Crowdfunding:** Using various platforms, like Kickstarter, Indiegogo, or Crowdfunding to start a project that will pay for your reviews. See book, "Publish Your Knowledge" page 43.

11.) **Book Clubs:** A team of likeminded individuals create a book club and through that club you get reviews.

12.) **Run a competition:** You can enter a competition and leave a review and you will win an Amazon gift-card for 50 dollars.

Example - Send me a link to review and I will send you a free book. This is usually run from the author's blog.

13.) **Mailing List** – send free stuff and reader list is obliged to write a review – I got all this free stuff, so I feel obliged to give something in return. See the free webinar screenshot example.

I absolutely loathe these Internet Hucksters/aka Marketers who are really profiting off you and me (if we take the bait).

Example Webinar

Here is my usual The **Good, Bad or Ugly** table.

My Good, Bad, or Ugly rating: Ugly	Why?
	-The 13 ways to get reviews I listed above; they are all asking for reviews (except #2 & #6)
	-People are compensated, or get something for FREE to provide a review in return
	-#6 is the only good way to get a review if it's not asked for

How to Spot Fake Reviews

"We all need people who will give us feedback. That's how we improve." -*Bill Gates*

Myle Ott and Jeff Hancock wrote a decent paper on, "**Estimating the Prevalence of Deception in Online Review Communities.**"

Their dataset included online review communities, such as: Expedia, Hotels.com, Orbitz, Priceline, TripAdvisor, Yelp and Mechanical Turk.

The paper concluded, among other findings that review communities with low posting requirements have high exposure to deceptive reviews.

As you will see in Amazon Review Eligibility, this could be one way that deceptive reviews posted on Amazon are minimized.

With that being said, Amazon still has a large population of fake reviews.

Know this: **greater than 50% of reviews are fake** on Amazon and other websites that sell products. To be more polite, these reviews were obtained by asking for them in various forms.

John Dough say's in his book, "*Fake Amazon Reviews*" over 95% of book reviews are fake, good, or bad.

This is just the game of one upping each other that was created and must be played if anyone is publishing on here and wants to get any traction for their book.

Link to the complete Amazon review: https://tinyurl.com/y64vk35w

Authentic Rating Rule: The only real **authentic review** is a review that has not been asked for, whether that is a good or bad review. There is no exception to that rule in my book!

As I said before, over 50% of reviews written online are fake. That includes the **good reviews** and the **bad reviews**. This is the game that is played by some to get ahead of the competition.

Some say it's as much as 95%. Source: **Self Publishers Must Read! Fake Amazon Reviews – 2ND edition, by Jon Dough.**

Fake Reviews can be 4 or 5-stars reviews, or they can be 1 or 2-star reviews. The review ratings for fake reviews are all dependent on the rater's motives. What's a good review then?

Look at the 3-star reviews first.

If the fake reviewer is working as a **Shill** (see glossary), their motive might be to write the review based on a payment by a publisher, or other self-published author.

This is ultimately how **they profit from 1-star reviews**. How? A publisher will look for a new niche to open on a book topic, say: Covid-19, or maybe vaccines.

They then wait for the author, publisher to accumulate their reviews. This is how the they validate it's a niche worth pursuing. They then publish a book in the same niche with a similar title.

The publisher will then employ their Shills to drop 1-star reviews on their competition. While the competition's sales tank, the book's replacement is now selling like hot-cakes!

After reading 3-star reviews, you should then look at 1 or 2-star reviews.

They usually include words, like: **This is more of a pamphlet than a book**, or similar words. Like, **this was not what I was looking for**.

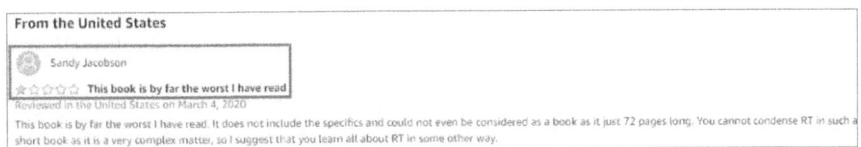

This person, "Sandy Jacobson" dropped 5 1-star reviews on one author's book. All of them were hidden on their profile. Just click on the name and it shows you their reviews.

Sandy's profile only shows 5 Star reviews.

Fake reviews written by shills will have many accounts, and they typically write 1 review per product, per Amazon account.

What is the Solution for these Shill 1 Star Reviews?

Unfortunately, there is not much you can do. The Shills know that. You can contact Amazon, but unless your name is **Hillary Clinton**, they will not remove the review.

What else can you do? You can get more good reviews, like 3, 4, or 5 star written reviews. That will help change your average score back to what you previously had.

Online Fake Review Tools

If you don't know how to read fake reviews, you can use an online authenticity review site, like: fakespot.com. Their site algorithm is not 100% accurate though.

Another site you may look at is reviewmeta.com.

Here is how I read reviews. I first look at the 1-star reviews and work my way up to the 3-star reviews. The 3-star reviews are probably the closest authentic reviews you can read and trust.

Let me give you an example of a Product Review. I will review which ones are most likely to be genuine.

Product: HiMoliwa Winter Gloves Touch Screen Fingers Skiing Gloves Men Women (XL, Black)

Average Customer Reviews: 3.9

16 Ratings (Includes written reviews)

Verified Ratings: 9 (4 Global)

Early Reviewer Rewards: 4

Vine Customer Review of Free Product: 2 (1 x 4 star and 1 x 1 star)

Rating Only 4 (2 Star)

5-star Reviews (4)

4-star Reviews (2)

3-star Reviews (2)

2-star reviews (0) – has a 2-star rating

1-star reviews (1)

Percentage Breakdown of Ratings

5 Star = 48%

4 Star = 20%

3 Star = 14%

2 Star = 9%

1 Star = 8%

Most Critical Review (1 Star)

I read some of the other reviews and it almost seems like people aren't all receiving the same gloves. The gloves I received are not warm at all, they have a very thin, fake fur lining that is comfortable, but only warm enough for a 55 degree or so fall day. The black material is smooth and very thin, it does nothing to add any warmth at all. They are also two sizes too small - I ordered these for my husband, who normally wears a large and these XL gloves barely fit me. (I wear a Medium). I definitely wouldn't recommend these as warm winter gloves, as they are advertised.

Top Critical Review (3 Star)

These are most definitely women's gloves. That black along the wrists is frilly, and the color/design does seem a tad feminine but I'm not a fashion designer so take that with a grain of salt.

Didn't wear but once, so I can't speak about the quality. Seemed nice enough. Gave it 3 stars because I didn't know what to put. They warn you about this so it isn't too bad, but you will definitely need a size to a size and a half bigger than normal if your hands are anything but slim.

Return process was easy.

Top positive review

We bought these gloves for a snowboarding trip to Colorado. We even went snowmobiling in them. They are waterproof and keep your hands warm. The touch screen finger was great. Did not have to take of my glove in the freezing cold to take picks of my family. (**Unverified**)

Odd that Amazon doesn't show the most critical review. Instead it shows the "**top critical review**".

Based on my experience, the top critical review is typically the review you should pay attention to. Where does it appear? That's the review that should show up to the right of the favorable review.

Example below.

To get the positive review and critical review page of an eBook. Click on the filter by verified purchase. Then filter on 3-star only.

Fakespot.com Review Grade: B

Fakespot Most Authentic Review: We bought these gloves for a snowboarding trip to Colorado.

As you can read the Fakespot robot (algorithm) selected the review that is probably not authentic. Why is not authentic? First, it's not a Verified Review (no verified rating badge). Secondly, it's not specific enough to warrant the 5 Star review rating.

The rating when compared to the most critical review doesn't seem like it is the same product? Which one is more authentic to you?

For me the review from *Ian* and *GP Alaska* are the best authentic reviews.

They explain several issues with the product. These are: Not warm at all; Too Small; and seem to be a female design (not for men).

The Amazon 3.9 Rating seems to be fair, based on the number of reviews and the actual rating break-out by percentage.

There are still other pieces of the puzzle to consider. How many reviews has Ian written? Ian has written 1, at the time of writing this.

GP Alaska has written greater than 2000. I bet you are more likely to go with GP Alaska's review.

Especially as he got the product at no cost. Just needs Amazon to declare this as income to Uncle Sam when the 1040 is filed.

How many people do all this research before buying the product? Not many I would bet.

The History of Amazon Reviews

Most people will probably not know this, but **Amazon started the very process of writing reviews** which is not allowed today and is against their terms and conditions.

Link to those terms are here: Click Me

Amazon team members (small number) would literally pay hundreds of writers to write reviews on books.

Essentially the reviews would be biased, as the writers were paid to write the reviews. It's been proven that those that are incentivized & writing reviews, will never write authentic reviews.

Look to the Amazon Vine Program, as an example. No money is exchanged, but the reviewer gets the product for FREE and in return the product owner will get a written review.

In fact, whoever started the company, allegedly according to the internet and legacy news media, it was **Jeff Bezos**. The company started with an idea that is very different today.

I totally understand why some consumers, absolutely hate Amazon! They destroyed and disrupted so many business models and well know American brand supply-chains.

A certain famous person was always talking about Amazon and USPS.

I bet when the company was started the instructions, were: Get me reviews, I don't care how you do it, but just get me f**king reviews, or you are fired!

Today authentic reviews are still hard to get and find, but there are still many people working around the terms and conditions.

You can read more about the history in this Amazon book - https://www.amazon.com/Everything-Store-Jeff-Bezos-Amazon/dp/0316377554

Just keep in mind that the book link above is written by a pre-qualified source. What do I mean? They are in the family! I will leave it at that.

What does Best Seller mean on Amazon?

The Amazon Best Sellers Rank (BSR), also known as the "Amazon Sales Rank" is a score that Amazon assigns a specific product.

It ranks a product based on sales and historical sales data and fluctuates hourly.

You can tell if an Amazon Kindle LinkedIn eBook is a best seller by this the orange Best Seller Label. Like the one below.

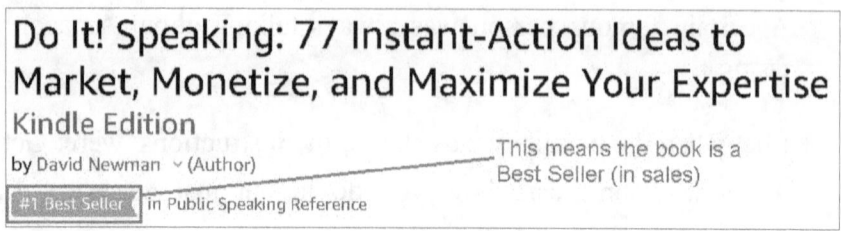

Link to Amazon Kindle Top 100 eBooks.

https://www.amazon.com/Best-Sellers-Kindle-Store/zgbs/digital-text

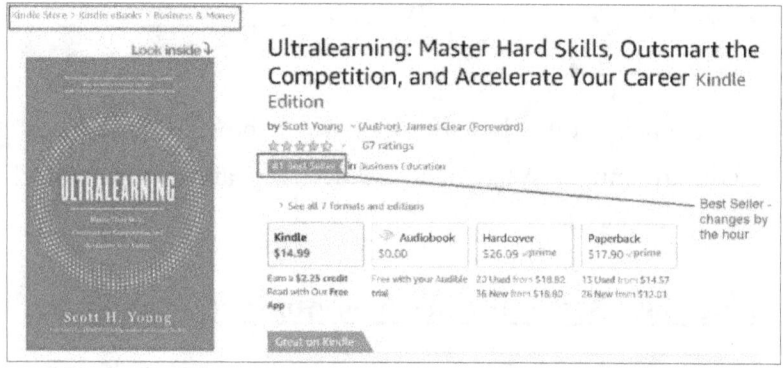

There is another orange label you should pay attention to as well - #1 New Release. This is the same as Best Seller.

However, one slight difference – the book is also a new release and was launched on Amazon within the last 30 days.

What are book categories?

To find a book, it must be listed in a category. It's the same if you go into a library, or you walk into a bookstore.

Each brick and mortar space will use a categorization system to help staff find the book and the same process is used in the digital age today.

In the digital age you can find on Amazon.com or Amazon.co.uk, an index and a category. This is required to rank the eBook for its customers.

Let me show you how, this is done using the LinkedIn eBook with the highest number of sales, currently.

What are some of the other badges, or labels you see on Amazon? There are two types of labels. One for written reviews and the other is about the listing publication, or chart position.

I will start with the review badges. Pay attention to these, as they impact the review's authenticity. Well at least it is better than nothing!

Written Review Badges

Verified Review

This means the reviewer purchased the product or book.

Vine Customer Review of Free Product

Pretty straight forward what this means. The review was incentivized by receiving a free product, or book in exchange for a review.

Early Reviewer Rewards

Customers who have purchased a product participating in the Early Reviewer Program may be asked to write a review and those customers who submit a review within the offer period will receive a small reward (e.g. a $1-$3 Amazon.com Gift Card) for helping future shoppers.

For more information click, or tap here.

Listing Publication Badges

New Release

This means the eBook has just been released and the author will get 30 days of FREE promotion on Amazon via that badge. It will be listed among other new releases with a ranking number attached.

Effectively you could get #1 New Release on day one if you have implemented a great marketing plan.

Amazon Charts

This means the eBook has been selected The Top 20 Most Sold & Most Read Books of the Week.

Just Released

The book has been published on Amazon in the last month or so.

You need to scroll down to the Product details section to see the publication date. The date is usually listed next to the publisher name.

How to Read a Kindle eBook Product Page

Amazon is **constantly** updating their Kindle eBook pages, so you need to know where to look. Here is a list of what you can review as a potential Kindle eBook buyer.

Look Inside

Before you look inside an eBook and read the first 10%, you need to make sure you have selected the Kindle eBook you are interested in.

For example, you should see: *Kindle > Kindle eBooks >Business & Money* (assuming you are looking in that section).

Click on the cover of the eBook and you can read the 1st 10% of the eBook for FREE. If the eBook has been setup correctly then you will start off with the cover inside the eBook.

Sometimes you will end up starting in a different location – blame the publisher if you do not!

What else can you do?

You can read the table of contents. You can download a sample of the eBook to your Amazon Kindle device, cloud reader, or mobile device.

When you have reached the end of the 10% of the eBook, you will see these words.

End of this sample Kindle book.
Enjoyed the preview?
Buy with 1-Click

or
See details for this book in the Kindle Store

Under the Book Title

Under the Book Title you will be able to see the author's name, how many ratings and if the eBook is a Best Seller.

If it's a Best Seller in one book category only, it will show the category that the eBook is listed in. This will be clickable, so you can see other similar books in that book search category.

Now if you click the book category, it's quite possible that the eBook is no longer number 1 in the book category. Amazon updates its Best-Seller rankings every hour.

The book category you clicked on will show the first 50 eBooks. Page 2 will be the other 50. Scroll through all of them to see what is on the list.

Wish List

You can add the eBook to your Amazon wish list. This is a list that you may create or use the default public list. **Authors appreciate you adding their eBooks to your lists**, as it impacts their book ranking.

Here is my public Amazon Wish List -
https://www.amazon.com/hz/wishlist/ls/newwl?ref_=wl_share

There will be nothing in it, as I don't use that list. All my books I want to read go into my private reading list.

Reading Reviews

Start reading the negative reviews first. Look for the words that indicate the eBook rater hasn't read the eBook. Then move up to the 2 stars, then 3 stars and so forth.

After about 5-10 minutes you should have a good idea which reviews resonate with you the most.

If you are still not sure check the Amazon Author Profile and see what they have written about themselves. You can even check other eBook titles that the author may have written.

Scroll up to the top of the eBook product page and the author name will be a hyperlink. When you click on the name it should take you to their author page.

Current user interface design requires you to click twice.

If there is no link, then the author hasn't setup their Amazon author page, which could be a red flag. A red flag that indicates the author may be a huckster.

Also compare and scrutinize the publication date with the date of the review. Were all the reviews posted before the book was published, or were they published on the same day, same week?

All these same day review dates could be an indicator of fake reviews – not authentic!

Ratings v Reviews

What are ratings? Ratings are basically where the consumer has tapped a button on their mobile device to indicate the 1-5-star rating.

Reviews are ratings with written reviews about the book, or product.

Note: You cannot leave a rating on non-mobile devices. The product page will only have a link to the "Write a customer review".

What's a Good Review Score?

From my experience of writing reviews since 2000, an authentic product review score is around 4.0 to 4.7. Anything higher than that, the reviews may be suspect.

Remember, less than 5% of buyers will leave a review.

Here is what "Neil" said at Quora –

- The customer review percentage though can vary dramatically and depends on things such as (in rough importance order).

- How many reviews does the product have currently? If it has none then the feedback rates are higher, but this decreases rapidly as the number of reviews increase. Greater than 10 reviews and people don't see the value of adding their opinion...

- How controversial or high profile the item is. The higher the profile then the more feedback it will get, thus outstripping its actual sales. Kindles, political biographies by controversial figures are all examples of this as the review forum essentially comes a debating space (much to the annoyance of those who want a balance view on the book)

- Also, whether or not a product has marketing reviews (it does happen) can impact the total number of reviews
- Enrollment in Amazon's vine program (reviews of free samples by top Amazon reviewers) will also impact the total

Why are there so many fake reviews on Amazon?

Many of the books sold on Amazon are written as big business cards and are just ways to get your email address.

The internet marketers use a book to sell you everything they can until you finally decide to delete your email address or remove your email from their marketing list.

What I find ironic is that a lot of nonfiction books sold on Amazon by self-published authors are actually more fiction than what is found in the fiction section!

Top Reviewers on Amazon

You can find a list of top customer reviewers here: https://www.amazon.com/review/top-reviewers

You can find the Amazon Hall of Famer reviewers here: https://www.amazon.com/hz/leaderboard/hall-of-fame

After looking at so many reviews over the years, a 4.6 overall rating and reviews from 1 through 5-star is a good indication that the eBook, or product has some authentic reviews.

Only a human can provide better detection than a bot.

The human eye is the best catch for spotting fake reviews and it takes years of writing reviews and reading them to learn that and make the process more automatic.

No thinking required.

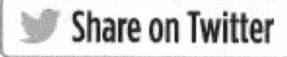

The Authentic Way to Get Reviews

This is one example of how a company called "pubby.co" has enabled a subscription pay wall to get reviews for books on Amazon.

Pubby is a book review service that launched in the Spring of 2019. Instead of paying per review or grabbing a spot on a long waitlist, authors simply earn points. The team at Pubby call them "snaps".

In exchange for reviewing other authors' books you earn snaps. The authors then use those snaps to get reviews for their own book.

Pubby say, it is typically a 1:1 ratio of writing a review to receive one in return.

Pubby Google Commercial

Here is what they say about themselves on Google: "Our Authors Get an Average of 3 Reviews in Their First 4 Days. Pubby Provides Authors with Visibility & Credibility.

No Waitlist. 10-Day Free Trial. Don't Pay Per Review. Fast Turnaround. Highlights: Anytime Cancellation Available, Individual Customer Support Available".

What is Pubby?

Pubby is an online membership website that allows authors of Amazon eBooks to get reviews.

How do you get reviews on Pubby?

To get reviews an author must collect "Snaps".

How do you access Pubby?

You can use my 15% discount link here: https://pubby.co/?invite=2582, or if you prefer you will access Pubby via this link: https://pubby.co, but no discount.

Authors that share their discount link can choose to receive Snaps in exchange for a new author signing up. Snaps are not received until a new author pays their monthly fee.

What types of Memberships are available?

There are 4 types of membership on offer from the outset. Established authors may have additional options for Premium based membership, which I detail below.

- 1 Book – 24.99 USD a month
- 4 Books – 39.99 USD a month
- 10 Books – 74.99 USD a month
- Unlimited Books – 124.99 USD a month
- Pubby Picks Standard - $179 USD – one-time payment
- Pubby Picks Professional - $349 USD – one-time payment

- Promotional Subscription - $29.99 USD a month

All of these offerings with the exception of Pubby Picks come with a 10-day FREE Trial.

You will of course have to cancel your subscription if any credit card has been shared in order not to be continually billed once the trial ends.

A note on unlimited

In my experience of using the Pubby Platform, unlimited is limited. What does that mean? This means **you can only review 8 books per week.**

Therefore, if you review 24 books in a month, which is the limit, so I would not even, consider the **Unlimited Books subscription** unless you work for a major publisher.

In which case that would be ironic, since Pubby is mainly aimed towards self-published authors!

A note on Pubby Picks

For both options all you are getting is extra snaps. Which means you can exchange them for reviews.

For Standard and Professional I would not use these, as I do not see them as good value, plus you are essentially paying for reviews.

Which is a **BIG RED FLAG** in this review book. **You should never pay for reviews.**

Even if this platform is setup to avoid triggering the **RED FLAG**. It's still doesn't meet my authentic review requirement.

Would I recommend Pubby?

Yes. **However, only for the first 1-5 reviews**. After that I would not use Pubby, as the best reviews are always from readers that are part of your tribe, or fan base.

Remember these are authors on Pubby who are primarily motivated to leave a review because they need reviews on their book(s).

If they do not leave reviews on other author books they will not earn "snaps"!

What is the Author's motivation to rate your book?

You can bet it will be different from a reader's motivation.

A reader will be motivated by what they love, like, or hate…they are not collecting "snaps" to get a review on a book.

You should be aware that less than 10% of readers read a book from cover to cover. Then inside that 10% bucket, even less leave a written review.

Probably that 2nd bucket is close to 1% who will leave a rating.

A Pubby author is primarily motivated in collecting snaps, so they can get more ratings of their book on Amazon.

Tell me more about collecting Snaps?

Let me answer that by explaining the way snaps are allocated purely based on reviewing author's books.

How many "Snaps" do you need for a single eBook review?

That depends, but here is the breakdown, as of December 2019.

- Standard Review: You need 1050 snaps
- Speedy Turnaround: You need an additional 400 snaps
- Verified Purchase: You need an additional 300 snaps
- 5-Star Rating Protection: You need an additional 300 snaps

For most of the eBook reviews I received, I used up 1350 snaps. That option includes the standard delivery, plus 300 snaps for a verified review.

One important note is that if your eBook is not priced at 0.99 USD and priced much higher; say 4.99 USD then the snaps required for a review/rating would be more.

For example, an eBook priced at 4.99 USD would be 1350 plus 300 plus 1500 snaps. That would be roughly 2500 snaps total for one eBook!

Pubby charges additional snaps based on the eBook price. Like so...

0.99 is 300 snaps; 1.99 is 600 snaps; 2.99 is 900 snaps; 3.99 is 1200 snaps and finally the 4.99 is 1500 snaps.

How do you get snaps from reading another Author's eBooks?

You make a request to read them and it is a 3-4 step process.

Step 1: Choose from Pubby' *limited* library of books, based on word-count, title, snaps received and turnaround

Step 2: After clicking on "Find a book" you can use a filter: Standard, Speedy, and or requires purchase

Step 3: Assuming you filtered on Standard, only the stand books will show up and the snaps received for these types of eBooks will be less than "Requires Purchase"

Click on the book you are interested in reading and rating.

You have to click on "start reading" You will already know how many snaps you will receive, as the advertising icon will show the number of snaps.

Standard snaps in this category would be 1000.

Then click on the start reading button.

Depending on the book setup, by the author and Pubby you will be presented with 3 options to tick. This is just a simple check-list box to tick etc.

Your options are:

Download this book (Standard setup only): usually comes in pdf, or ePub format. Be patient for the web server to send you the digital copy of the book to your device [notebook/Smartphone/pc, or tablet].

When you click the blue download book button, the pdf will automatically download and prompt you where you want to save it?

Then you just tick the boxes:

Download this book.

Read this book & summary and Post your review on Amazon.

There is an orange button which will allow you to copy the Amazon URL to another browser tab.

Click on "view on Amazon" the URL will then be copied to the clipboard. Paste the clipboard contents into a new browser tab. Like this one: https://www.amazon.com/dp/1701876752

Once you have read the eBook, you can then go back to Pubby and click on the Post your review on Amazon.

This is just a checklist item and it also tells Pubby to schedule a download of this review from Amazon to the Pubby platform later.

When you turn in your review you will be required to indicate the rating: 1 star to 5 stars and your Amazon Review Profile userid (this automatically gets filled-in). Then just click submit review.

You will instantly receive the Pubby snaps after you tap/or click on the Post your review on Amazon button.

Depending on the way the author setup their book for review you will get anywhere from 1 day to 4 days to complete the review. The 1st day includes the day you requested the eBook.

If you choose to cancel the book review, just go back to your Reader section in the left-hand frame of Pubby.co and click on the book, then on the right-hand side, click "Cancel Assignment"

Special Notice

One important note, which I often forget, is you should wait 6 hours before posting a review.

I have not followed this advice and noticed that for an eBook I purchased and left a review within 3 hours, the review does not show up.

Instead the review is listed without the "*Verified Purchase*" badge. If you want to do your reviews quickly, I recommend you download the eBook to your Amazon Kindle first.

Then post the review after 6 hours have elapsed. See the screenshot from the book assignment dashboard.

> **Your Todos**
>
> This assignment requires you to purchase the book on Amazon.com.
>
> You **cannot** use Kindle Unlimited to purchase this book for free because Amazon does not include those reviews as 'Verified Purchases'. If you wish not to purchase this book, click 'Cancel Assignment' on this page.
>
> Amazon may not approve your review if you post it immediately after purchasing the book. We recommend waiting at least **6 hours** after purchasing the book before posting your review.

How can you get additional Snaps?

Under the section Author – the left frame of the dashboard, if you scroll down you can see your *Snap Challenges*.

Below I list all the additional Snaps you may receive once you meet the current challenges set by the Pubby Platform founder/team.

How do you navigate around Pubby?

If you are accessing Pubby via app.pubby.co you will either go to Author or the Reader section. The other areas you can review are:

Notifications – this shows the alerts like, when you submit one of your books to be reviewed, or when you added a book you will read and review.

Account settings – takes you through your Pubby account settings

Contact Support (Pubby) – this will bring up the chatbot. Remember since this is a "bot" the responses are pre-curated until a live human comes online, like Kristen Forbes the founder.

What type of books are on Pubby?

Most books I have seen listed are fiction books. There are some non-fiction books, but since November 2019 I have not seen many books submitted.

For example: Undercover Debutante, Such Unfortunates; The Legend of Colgan Toomey; Mind of a Madmen; The White Spider of Savignac; Kill Crime; Galactic Passages Planet 6333; The True Nature of Human Nature; Princess Sparkle Fang and the Fairy Mischief.

How do you submit your book to Pubby?

Assuming you have signed up for the membership, here are the steps you are taken through.

There are roughly 13 steps/fields you need to complete.

Step 1: Under the Author Section, click or tap on "Add Book"

Step 2: Provide the Title of the book and the Author of the book – these should be the same as on your book cover, or front-matter. The click the continue button

Step 3: Then choose your reader types. These are: Standard; Kindle Unlimited; and Verified Purchases.

I always only add the latter two: Kindle Unlimited and Verified Purchases (requires one-time fee). After you tick the box for what type of reader review (ratings) you wish for your book, click the button continue

Step 4: Upload your book cover. I always use the book cover I have currently loaded on the Amazon bookstore. Pubby allows the following formats: jpg; png; and gif

Step 5: Once you have uploaded your cover, two more fields will appear. Enter the US Amazon book URL, like this one: https://www.amazon.com/dp/B01N5EUNWW

You can choose to use the Kindle URL, or the paperback URL – depending what you have created in the product store of Amazon

Step 6: Submit the Genre of your book. This is a pre-populated list you select from. I typically choose: Business. At this point you should be 70% complete. For some reason if you choose the

Genre of the book, your Amazon URL gets blanked out, which puts you back to 60%. Just recopy the URL in if you see this issue when setting your book up for reader review

Step 7: Choose the Phrases that describe your book: The list of these are below:

a well-written page turner.

Step 8: Summarize the book in two or more sentences. An easy way to complete this is to copy review information that you already have on your book. That's assuming you have at least on review already!

Step 9: What is unique about the book and sets it apart from others? This is self-explanatory, but if there are any other books like yours you want to describe what is unique about your creative offering.

Step 10: What do you believe readers will enjoy most about the book? Put two or three words together to describe what the reader will like. For example, Real world examples.

Step 11: Fill in the blank: Fans of the book(s) _____ will enjoy this book. This one is the most confusing section that you need to fill-in. I have seen multiple uses for this field. However, you are supposed to put in there any books that are similar that you like, and you feel that the reader may like too.

Step 12: Please copy and paste your favorite excerpt(s) or recipe(s) from the book below. Just open your eBook or paperback manuscript and copy 1 or 2 paragraphs from your work into this field.

You can also go to your online reviews where a reader has quoted your book etc. You will then have an endorsement that shows what other readers like.

Step 13: What other information would you like to give potential readers about the author or the book? More of the same as in step 12. You can just add extra information about your work here.

Now you should be 100% complete, and the Pubby tool will enable the Submit for Approval button. Click, or tap that blue button! Kristen says it usually gets approved within 4 hours.

Keep in mind that Kristen is a busy person, so it may take the whole 4 hours to get it approved. I submitted one book over Thanksgiving Holiday, and it took more than a day to get approved.

So timing is everything when it comes to getting your book up on Pubby, ready for the Amazon Raters to do their great work for you and your book!

Where does your submitted Book go? You can see your submitted book under the author section. It should say: Your Book Title – Pending Approval in green and then alongside that – Approved within 4 hours.

If you get distracted and come back without finishing the book setup, Pubby saves your work, so you can continue where you left off. This is a great feature.

Depending on the book you are adding to be reviewed it takes on average 15 to 30 minutes to complete. Of course, you can setup your book in less time once you have gone through this process at least once.

That is the end of the example.

How do you get help?

Pubby has an online chatbot. When you enter a request, you are at the mercy of the co-founder being available to respond. Sometimes, in my experience you do not get any response.

Be warned.

From my own experience, the membership fee does not go towards staffing the chatbot with humans. It seems that Kristen is the only one managing the site. See screenshots below.

Where are the Book Reviewers Located?

All in the USA. For all the reviews I looked at, the reviewer's Amazon account is in the USA. Perhaps Kristen the co-founder can confirm that?

Is there a Help Library?

No there isn't but most of the platform is straight forward. I needed help when I submitted a book without requiring the verified review button for review.

This meant I could not submit the book for verified review. Once I realized this, I edited the book and re-submitted (after paying 14.99 USD) a one-time charge for the feature.

When you click the help button on the left side of the user interface it brings up the chatbot interface.

There is also a yellow icon on the other side of your screen that brings up the same interface.

What do I recommend?

I recommend you plan what you want to get out of Pubby before you sign-up. Write down what you believe to be a reasonable goal. You should set it for 30 days.

I know from all the research I have done in 20+ years, roughly 10% of the USA population read books. That doesn't mean they read it from cover to cover either!

If your book(s) are not in the top 10% of sales **it doesn't matter how many reviews you pay for** (indirectly), your precious work is not going to make money for you.

What is your budget for the written reviews? Is it $100 USD, or less? That might make it easier for you to decide how to leverage the Pubby platform for Authors to get ratings.

Who is Kristen Forbes?

Before becoming the founder (previously co-founder) of the Pubby platform for authors, Kristen, according to her LinkedIn BIO, is, or was working as a publisher/book editor for various firms.

You can view her LinkedIn profile here: Kristen Forbes.

Previously, her LinkedIn profile says she was the owner and editor of Deviance Press. However, her LinkedIn tagline said at the time of viewing it: **Owner of DeviancePress.com & pubby.co**

Here is my usual, Good, Bad or Ugly review table.

My Good, Bad, or Ugly rating: Good	Why?
	-It's the best way self-published authors can get authentic reviews -But there is a catch, authors are paying for a subscription, so is it good or bad? -It is probably bad, because of the money, but it does not violate Amazon's terms and conditions, so let's say it's good! -There is a > certainty that the review is written better than most

As you can see, I like Pubby! It's the closest you can get to an authentic review without violating the Amazon terms and conditions.

What are you waiting for, check it out here: Pubby.co, or use my 15% discount link - https://pubby.co/?invite=2582

8 Easy Ways to Support Your Favorite Author

Amazon Social Media Support

Here are the recommended steps. Login to Amazon.com or Amazon.co.uk with your userid (your email) and password.

Positive Sentiments [Ratings]

1. Pick your favorite eBook to review and click the rating button

2. Go through the entire **3, 4, & 5-star reviews**, and then click on Yes, as below

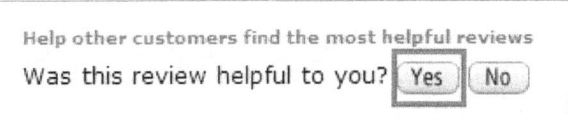

3. Then click this link: http://amzn.to/17lBttR

4. Click on the "**Follow**" button on the left under the headshot

5. Buy the paperback for a friend

6. Tweet a link out to my author page by hitting the Twitter icon!

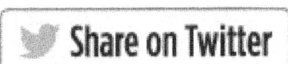

Thanks so much for your help in socializing my **The Good, Bad and Ugly Reviews** http://amzn.to/12pyCNu Kindle eBook and **Paperback book!** http://amzn.to/1aEvS2U

If you bought this eBook, don't forget to leave your review for others to benefit from your review!

7) Sometimes when reader's finish their book the information is not communicated back to Amazon Cloud Servers, so help author's by marking it as read. Here is how. Go to this link (after you login) and click, or tap http://www.amazon.com/mycd

Then select the content tab. A list of all your Kindle content should be displayed. Highlight a row and then click Mark as read.

That will help Amazon give author's credit for their eBooks listed on Amazon.com

8) Lastly, add the entire author's book inventory to your wish list - http://amzn.to/1llLWsw (USA, UK, etc.)

TIP: If you are an author and you ask for a review, when you receive it go back to the review and click the "Helpful" button.

That will help the reviewer too. The reviewer may climb in the Amazon Review Rankings.

Link to ranking here: https://www.amazon.com/reviews/top-reviewers

The more helpful votes they get, the higher they get in the Amazon Review Rankings.

Thank you so much!

Note: You must have an Amazon account and have spent $50 in the last 12 months to be eligible for posting a review. The amount in the UK is 40 pounds.

In Conclusion

Why did I write this eBook? Well, that my friend this is easy to explain for me.

After writing my first book in 2012, which was making more money than I anticipated, and then another that was a best-seller for 3 years in a row in a niche where I had no academic experience.

Still that book is doing well. Sales typically increase at the end of the year and the first 3 months of the year, which is understandable, as it is to do with family legacy planning.

If you are interested, you can find it here: Build Your Own Living Revocable Trust: A Pocket Guide to Creating a Living Revocable Trust - http://mybook.to/byotrust

All that was great for a new author, who did not know how self-publishing worked at the time of publishing back then in 2014.

Then sales started to dwindle. I had to find out why, and through researching why, this eBook with all the data I collected was born.

I wanted to share my experience with others, to give back what I know to be true via my own personal experience.

First off, famous authors do not play by the rules. Famous authors, in some cases do not even write their own books.

If you still think that James Patterson, J. K. Rowling, Bill Clinton, Hillary Clinton, Tim Ferriss, and many other authors write their own books, then I cannot help you my friend.

Let's take just one example from that list of people I quoted in the previous sentence. **Hillary Clinton** – her last book, what was it again?

Kudos if you know the title before I search to find out what the name of the book was...

Guess what, I had to look up the book, the title of the book is: **What Happened**

Oh yea, "What Happened". Aptly named!

No punctuation included. The first day it was published there was almost 1000 reviews submitted to Amazon that were 1-star reviews.

I reviewed a few of them and what I noticed in addition to the slamming of the publication was they were literally disappearing as fast as they were appearing!

Right now, the review rating is 4.7. The 1-star reviews are at about 4%. 5 Star review are at 79%. Total global ratings are at 6.367. That's a lot of ratings!

My point is that once you have a famous name, connections, a publishing company, called Simon & Schuster, you can easily influence things to "appear" or change in your favor.

Here is a link to one of the stories that broke via mainstream media – https://mashable.com/2017/09/14/hillary-clinton-what-happened-amazon-reviews/

I am not a judge or a jury on what you decide to do going forward.

However, what I want you to take away from spending time reading this book is that the world of publishing is not what you have been programmed to believe.

There is a **review illusion** you must learn to see through.

For example, the best book I have read on this **book review topic** is not even on sale anymore!

If you are an author take the Terms and conditions with a pinch of salt. Don't mis-interpret the rules! Remember, Jeff Bezos is not who you think he is.

Recall, the company started the company by paying people to write book reviews!

For potential future readers, not just this eBook, but many others from self-published authors, please help them grow.

You can do that by following the recommendations I made in this section: How to help Authors.

Remember, next time you are thinking of buying a book, or product on Amazon, review the 3-star, then 2-star and 1-star reviews. Reviews are worth more to the author than ratings!

Get Lifetime Updates of This eBook

"What you do not want done to yourself, do not do to others."
-**Confucius**

Secret Applicable to any Amazon eBook

Once you have learned and applied what you discover in this section of the eBook you can get lifetime updates of <u>any</u> Amazon eBook published on the Amazon platform.

The only restriction will be if Amazon stops selling eBooks! Here are the steps to get to the form below.

How to Get Lifetime Updates

1) Click this link: https://kdp.amazon.com/en_US/contact-us

2) Click Pricing

3) Type in New Kindle Version for **Subject Title**

4) Type in the ASIN, in this case it would be:

5) Type in this for the Description of issue / inquiry:

I already own, insert ASIN: The author has informed me that the eBook has been revised. Please send me the latest version to my Kindle eBook library

6) Say thanks for your help

7) Then click the submit button

Once you have submitted the request you will see the below response.

Thank you! We've received your message. You should expect a response within 24 hours. In some cases, our reply may take longer as we research your inquiry.

See screenshot for how the form submission process looks like on the Amazon.com USA site.

Note: It usually takes 12-24 hours to get a response. If you do get a response, but the Amazon agent does not send you the latest version, just reply to the email and ask again.

Here is their email address if you don't wish to use the form: kdp-support.amazon.com

Sometimes the agent is new and does not know how to send new content to you, the eBook reader/customer.

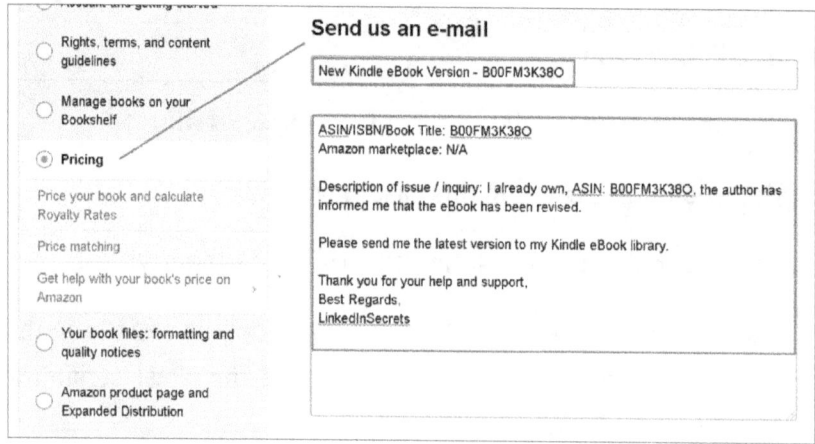

That is, it. Now you can apply this secret tip to any eBook that has been revised and **has the same ASIN.**

You can easily tell which version you have purchased of my eBooks, as I put the version information at the front of the eBook.

Just compare what's on the Amazon store to what you have in your Kindle library.

With the thousands of books out there, you will find few authors out there that will update their books as often as I do.

Sources - Further Reading And Products For Review

I put this list together based on my research for this eBook and for further reaching. This information will further backup what I am telling you about reviews on Amazon.

1. Free Amazon Items by writing FAKE reviews– The Frugal Analyst, https://youtu.be/KrGTkjA8D2M
2. Amazon and the problem of fake reviews, https://youtu.be/eDrK7qKFU1Y
3. Kindle Best-seller list, https://www.amazon.com/Best-Sellers-Kindle-Store-eBooks/zgbs/digital-text/154606011/ref=zg_bs_nav_kstore_1_kstore
4. How to Get a Truckload of Reviews on Amazon.com, https://www.amazon.com/gp/product/B00GJA9K8S
5. NAKED TRUTHS About Getting Book Reviews 2018, https://www.amazon.com/NAKED-TRUTHS-About-Getting-Reviews-ebook/dp/B0792BRRBQ
6. How to Write a Simple Book Review: It's easier than you think, https://www.amazon.com/gp/product/B015FQ85SW
7. How to find Book Reviewers, https://www.amazon.com/gp/product/B01B2TP0Z2

8. Get Reviews so You Can Sell More Books: 20 Good, Bad and Questionable Tips for Amazon's Review System (How to Sell More Books), https://www.amazon.com/Get-Reviews-Sell-More-Books-ebook/dp/B00GFSCLVM

9. Kindle Reviews: How to Get More Reviews for Your Kindle Book. (Write Free Book Series), https://www.amazon.com/Kindle-Reviews-More-Book-Write-ebook/dp/B01CDKRPSY

10. How to Write a Book Review: A Simple Book Review Template Anyone Can Learn, https://www.amazon.com/How-Write-Book-Review-Template-ebook/dp/B08B4XYWD7

11. The Everything Store: Jeff Bezos and the Age of Amazon, https://www.amazon.com/Everything-Store-Jeff-Bezos-Amazon-ebook/dp/B00BWQW73E

12. How to get Amazon Reviews without getting Suspended in 2020, https://youtu.be/U2tcP6PFZm0

13. The War to Sell You A Mattress Is an Internet Nightmare, Forbes 2017

14. In a Race to Out Rave, 5Star Web Reviews Go for $5, New York Times, August 9, 2011

15. Finding Deceptive Opinion Spam by Any Stretch of the Imagination, Claire Cardie, June 2011

16. Cracking the code on Amazon Fake Reviews…, https://www.amazon.com/dp/B01MSXU56L

17. Online Reputation Management (2020): Secrets from a Pro Ethical Hacker,
    https://www.amazon.com/dp/B07BWDDN13

18. Amazon's murky world of one-star reviews,
    https://www.bbc.com/news/technology-54063039

19. A Statistical Analysis of 1.2 Million Amazon Reviews,
    https://minimaxir.com/2014/06/reviewing-reviews/

20. Review Summarizer (Apps, Electronics),
    https://thereviewindex.com/us

21. The Ghost Writer,
    https://www.amazon.com/dp/B009HEIHZA

22. How to leave a review on Amazon,
    https://www.youtube.com/watch?v=wc4t4elNAmI

23. How to fight negative reviews on Amazon,
    https://www.orderhive.com/how-to-fight-negative-reviews-on-amazon

24. Local Consumer Review Survey,
    https://www.brightlocal.com/research/local-consumer-review-survey/

25. How to get Book Reviews on Amazon (Authentically)…,
    https://www.amazon.com/How-Book-Reviews-Amazon-Authentically-ebook/dp/B08XPNRCWV

Recommended Websites for Further Review

Web: **16 Best Selling LinkedIn eBooks of all time,**
https://bookauthority.org/books/best-selling-linkedin-ebooks

Web: **Say No to Fake Product Reviews,**
https://www.fakespot.com/

Web: **ReviewMeta.com analyzes Amazon product reviews and filters out reviews that look un natural,** https://reviewmeta.com/

Web: **How to Spot a Fake Review,**
https://www.wikihow.com/Spot-a-Fake-Review-on-Amazon

Web: **Tips to Spotting a Fake Review,**
https://www.cnbc.com/2019/07/12/prime-day-tips-for-spotting-a-fake-reviews-on-amazon.html

Web: **Amazon Community Guidelines,**
https://www.amazon.com/gp/help/customer/display.html?nodeId=201929730

Web: **Review and rate your Amazon Purchases,**
https://www.amazon.com/review/create-review/listing

Web: **Why does Amazon show more "Ratings" than ReviewMeta shows "Reviews"?,** https://reviewmeta.com/blog/why-does-amazon-show-more-ratings-than-reviewmeta-shows-reviews/

Web: **Unlimited Reviews for All Your Books, Free for 10 days**, https://pubby.co/

Web: **Amazon's Top Customer Reviewers**, https://www.amazon.com/review/top-reviewers

Web: **Step 1 to Selling You Book..**, https://www.entrepreneur.com/article/244881

Web: **Just pay shipping scam**, http://www.sellerdeck.co.uk/2017/09/04/the-just-pay-shipping-scam/

Web: **Five fake stars: Inside the black market of fake Amazon reviews**, https://youtu.be/XfVv7ZMSsl4

Web: **What is the Early Reviewer Program?**, https://www.amazon.com/gp/help/customer/display.html?nodeId=202094910&ie=UTF8

Web: **Amazon Vine Reviews**, https://www.nytimes.com/wirecutter/blog/lets-talk-about-amazon-reviews/#vine

Web: **What-percentage-of-buyers-write-reviews-on-Amazon**, https://www.quora.com/What-percentage-of-buyers-write-reviews-on-Amazon?

Web: **Customer Ratings vs Reviews**, https://sellercentral.amazon.com/forums/t/customer-ratings-vs-reviews/511634

Web: **Paid Amazon Book Reviews Continue Unabated**, https://justpublishingadvice.com/paid-amazon-book-reviews-continue-unabated/

Web: **Kindle Unlimited**, https://www.amazon.com/kindle-dbs/ku/ku-central

Web: **15% discount for Pubby**, https://pubby.co/?invite=2582

Web: **The Ghost Writer**, https://www.imdb.com/title/tt1139328/

Web: **Amazon Top Customer Reviewers**, https://www.amazon.com/review/top-reviewers

Web: **1-Star Reviews on Hillary's book**, https://mashable.com/2017/09/14/hillary-clinton-what-happened-amazon-reviews/

Web: **Book Marketing in 584 Words**, https://ckarchive.com/b/xmuph6ho5nol

Web, **Non-Fiction Writing Tips**, https://docs.google.com/document/d/1aIlom36LAERdmd5aKHLQFzA-MucEEZsjW3TyUnTnrWo/edit#

Web: **Why is feedback so worthless on Amazon?**, https://sellercentral.amazon.com/forums/t/why-is-feedback-so-worthless-on-amazon-buyer-fraud-mentality/749502

Amazon Terms & Glossary

Shill Review: A person who has an Amazon account that is paid to leave good reviews, or bad reviews.

Authentic Review: The review has been written by an Amazon customer who was not asked to leave the review, they bought the book, or product and are using it etc.

Fake Review: The review written is not authentic. It could be written by a competitor shill, or it was obtained via an email list. Another way the reviewer buys the product and gets a refund after leaving a review via PayPal.

Huckster: One who sells things of questionable value in an aggressive or dishonest manner.

Email List: An electronic mailing list or email list is a special use of email that allows for widespread distribution of information to many Internet users. **Source:** Wikipedia.

Ratings: This is where an Amazon customer has tapped on stars, after buying a product/book on Amazon. In this case writing a review is not necessary. The rating is shared via a mobile device.

Reviews: Similar to ratings, only the person writes about their experience with the product they purchased and rated it, using the Amazon 5-star rating system.

Verified Purchase: An *"Amazon Verified Purchase"* review means we've verified that the person writing the review purchased the product at Amazon and didn't receive the product for FREE

Early Reviewer Rewards: This person was compensated by Amazon for leaving a written review during the first month of sale. This is what Amazon states: "Customers who have purchased a product participating in the Early Reviewer Program may be asked to write a review and those customers who submit a review within the offer period will receive a small reward (e.g. a $1-$3 Amazon.com Gift Card) for helping future shoppers."

Ghost Writer: A ghostwriter is hired to write literary or journalistic works, speeches, or other texts that are officially credited to another person as the author.

Internet Marketer: Internet marketing is the process of promoting a brand or business and its products or services to customers through digital channels such as search engines, email, websites, and social media.

FBA: Fulfilled by Amazon. You can send your product, or books to an Amazon fulfillment center and get them to ship the order when it comes in.

Questions or Comments?

Congratulations for getting this far and reading this eBook! Now that you have read the eBook and put it to good use, I would love to hear <u>direct</u> from you.

You can send me a question via email address within this eBook. I usually read and reply to all my emails! If you prefer you can DM via Twitter at this link: https://twitter.com/linkedinsecrets

Just send me an email to: LinkedInSecretsRevealed@gmail.com – Subject: I read: The Good, Bad and Ugly of Product Reviews

Other Books by the Author

14 books previously published on various topics, including LinkedIn. Includes: Two prior Amazon Best Sellers. This is not the complete list of published books, but some of them are included here.

Top 10 LinkedIn Greatest Sellers: The Ultimate Top Ten LinkedIn eBooks (Volume Book 1) http://mybook.to/LinkedInBestSellers

Premium LinkedIn Profile: Career Subscription - Will it Land Your Next Job? http://mybook.to/PremiumLinkedIn

How to Bullet Proof Your LinkedIn Profile: 10 Security Issues to Avoid http://myBook.to/LinkedInSecurity

Pimp Your Profile: How to Amplify your LinkedIn Profile on your Mobile Device http://myBook.to/pyp

LinkedIn Secrets Revealed: 10 Secrets to Unlocking Your Complete Profile on LinkedIn.com
http://mybook.to/LinkedInSecrets

Write Your Book Outline: How to Create Your Book Outline in 30 Minutes http://myBook.to/outline

Publishing a Book on Amazon: 7 Steps to Publishing your #1 Book on Amazon Kindle in Minutes!
http://mybook.to/7StepsPublishing

Build Your Own Living Revocable Trust: A Pocket Guide to Creating a Living Revocable Trust http://mybook.to/byotrust

Spirituality in the Workplace: A Study Guide for Business Leaders http://amzn.to/1NHROA5

Amazon Secrets Revealed: How to Sell More Books on Amazon.com http://amzn.to/1Np2VaI

Email Inbox Management: How to Master Your Inbox with Etiquette http://mybook.to/MasterEmail

Love or Hate Email... 21 Rules to Change Your - I Must Check my Email Habit. Get Back to Work and Make Money Again! http://bit.ly/Love_Email

Trapped in a Meritocracy: Cracking the Meritocracy Code: Get Paid More for Valued Performance http://amzn.to/1zbufrW

Note: In most cases these links are to Amazon.com eBooks. Wherever possible the sales region is automatically detected. Some of the links sent to me may be Amazon affiliate links.

Now Please Share Your Opinion and Write a Review

One last thing, if you believe this book has helped you and is worth sharing with other potential Amazon Kindle readers; please leave a review by **clicking on the button** below.

Your review feedback will make the next version of this LinkedIn eBook even better for future readers.

[Create your own review]

https://amzn.to/2QuK8db

On Amazon, all 4-5 stars ratings are like gold! I would really appreciate you leaving a 4, or 5-star review - it should take only a few seconds of your time.

The button above is for the USA.

When you leave a 5-starreview, I feel like you have given me a gold bar like below!!

Thank You for reading and finishing this eBook!

About the Author

Patrick Gallagher provides his talent & services to various companies.

Throughout his multifaceted career, Patrick has received notable acclaim in the form of dozens of certifications and numerous awards.

Currently he is ranked in the top 5,000 of Amazon reviewers.

He has been writing reviews on Amazon since 2000.

This author was also a member of the Amazon Vine Program.

The Exclusive Club of Influential Amazon Voices.

https://www.amazon.com/gp/vine/review

You can find his Amazon Author Profile below:

http://author.to/LinkedInAuthor

★Return to Table of Contents★

www.ingramcontent.com/pod-product-compliance
Lightning Source LLC
Chambersburg PA
CBHW070653220526
45466CB00001B/423